'To my own children (Spencer & Lillian) who I will always want cuddles from.'
Aly

'For Celeste.'
Jason

Never Too Big For A Cuddle.

Copyright © Aly Walsh
Illustrations copyright © Jason Howe

First Edition 2015
Published by Aly's Books

www.alysbooks.com

Your Book | Our Mission

Designed by Jason Howe

design · fine art · illustration
DRAWNBYJASON.COM

Edited by Irrefutable Proof
www.irrefutable-proof.com

All rights reserved. No part of this book may be reproduced or transmitted in any form or by any means, electronic, mechanical, photocopying or otherwise without the prior permission of the publisher.

ISBN: 978-0-9941767-6-9

Never Too Big For A CUDDLE

written by **Aly Walsh** illustrated by **Jason Howe**

Are you as big **big big** as a GORILLA?

Then you are not too big big big
for a cuddle.

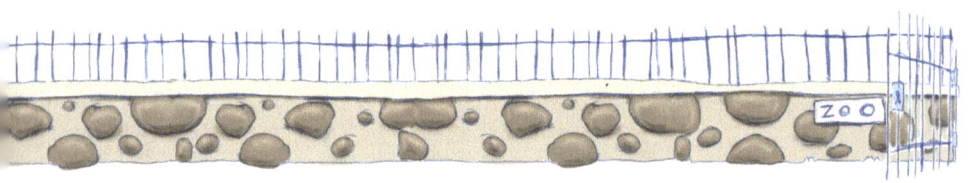 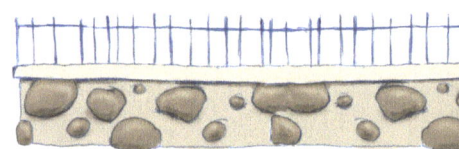

Are you as big big big as a GRIZZLY BEAR?

Then you are not too big big big
for a cuddle.

Are you as big big big as an ELEPHANT?

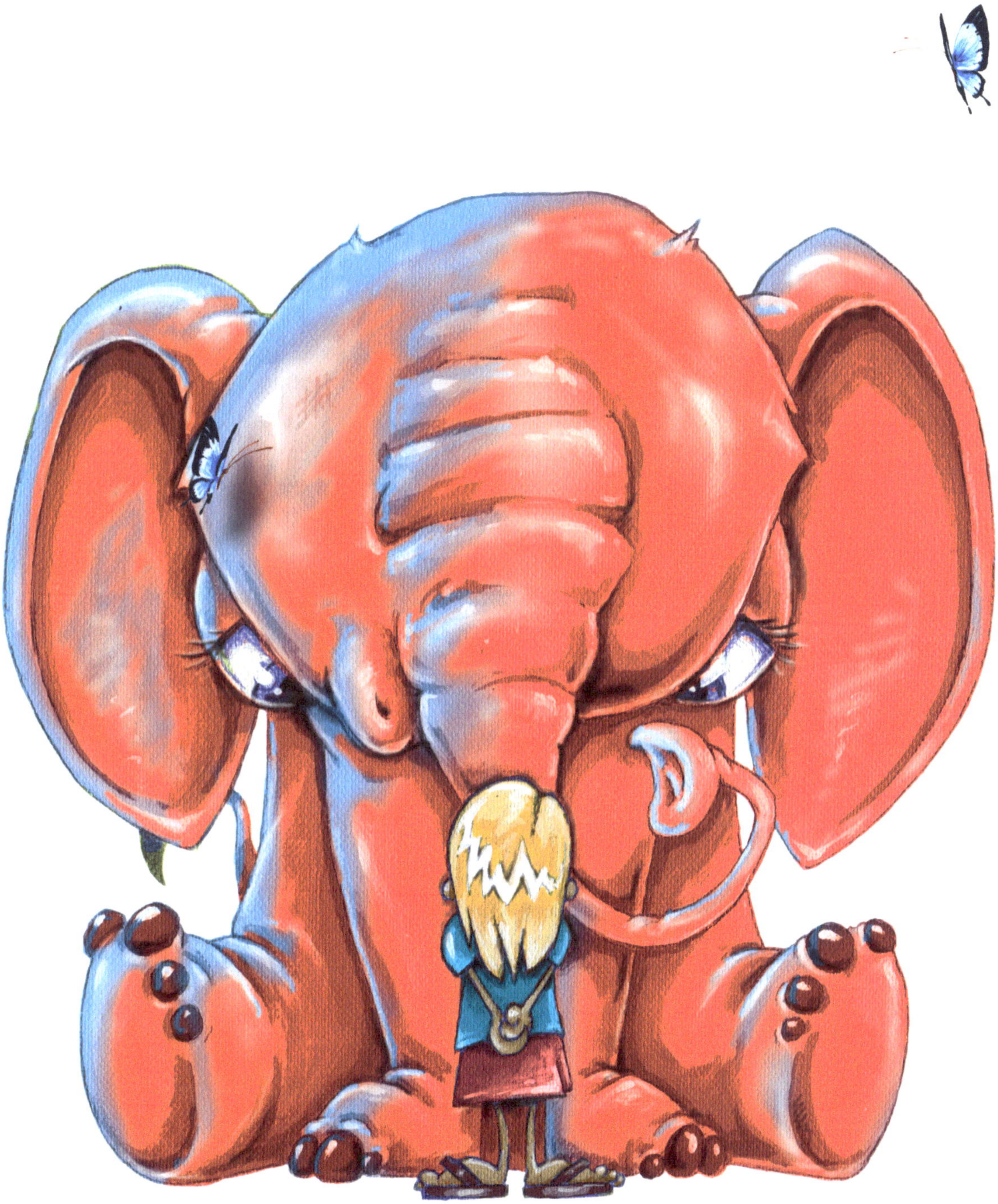

Then you are not too big big big
for a cuddle.

Are you as big big big as a DRAGON?

Then you are not too big big big for a cuddle.

Are you as big big big as a DINOSAUR?

Then you are not too big big big for a cuddle.

Are you as big big big
as a RAINBOW?

Then you are not too big big big for a cuddle.

Are you as big big big as the MOON?

Then you are not too big **big big** for a cuddle.

Even when you are big big big big big big big big **bigger** than your mum or dad, nana, pa, grandma, poppy

or your aunties and uncles and friends...

You will never be too big **big big** for a cuddle.

And guess who else is not too

'The following are people who have supported us and made this book possible. Thank you.'

Justin, Spencer & Lillian Walsh
Victoria Howe
The Howe's, Rintoul's & Lenarduzzi's
Isla Arnstein
Willow Ella Turner
Joseph, Elijah & Chiara
Odin & Matilda
Spencer Peattie
Ollie Jeffries
Jacob & Harrison Brink
Ava Ongarezos, Ava Rees & Harvey Briese
Freddy & Jasper Belton
Olivia, Harry & Ben Shannon
Elliot & Emma Whinnen
Tanisha & Zachary Zerafa
Lucas Klimis
Riley & Kenzi Watson
Paityn Fox
Sophie Mack
Oscar Brenan
Leo Kaandorp
Scout Whitla
Barry & Marilyn Walsh
Azura Smogavec, London Townsend
Isabella & Sebastien Sambell
James & Grace Marks
Yve, Rose & Allegra
Eliza & Madden Reynolds
Madeline & Lucas Mikhael
Lucrezia Chloe Hamilton
Millie Boothroyd, Zavier Carabott, Levi Tieppo, Eva English
Josh & Ben Pagan-Saunders
Katherine & Lauren H
Nathan & Max Giorlando
Justin, Erin & Eden Healy

Laura Porto
The Children at Alouette Eastlakes
Freddy Max Granger
Amy, Lana & Boyd Yates
Paige, Lauren & Rory Muller
Kai & Nate Allom
Tayla & Bella Nissen
Emily Kate & Joel James Telley
Violet Melnyk
Isla & Marlie Craig
Stephanie & David Everett
Ava & Gus Mollross
Ernie Brown
Dean, Steph, Faith & Archie Brown
Cristien Ethan & Maya Juliette Endekov
Daniel & April Yates
Sam & Gus Ernst
Tegan, Riley & Callum
Tom & Emily Walsh
Will Milton
Carlo & Ruby Sartinas
Sienna Grace Cooney
Zane Archer Hill
Ruby Morris
Max Krake
Josh Patterson
Zoe & Madison Clark
Alexander Demitriou
Kyle, Casey & Tristan Kilb
Barry Brown
Callan & Emily Thompson
Brown's, Walsh's and Cox's
Dan Ghys, Alexa Madison Ghys & Gwendlyn Mae Ghys
Diesel, Beau and Tilly
Hannah and Amber

www.ingramcontent.com/pod-product-compliance
Lightning Source LLC
Chambersburg PA
CBHW041125300426
44113CB00002B/63